I0465119

Body Love:
A Fat Activism Colouring Book

ALLISON TUNIS

Copyright © 2016, 2023 Allison Tunis

All rights reserved.

ISBN: 1523352779
ISBN-13: 978-1523352777

DEDICATION

To every person who has ever looked in the mirror and hated what they saw.
You do not have to feel like this.

ACKNOWLEDGMENTS

I would like to acknowledge all of the amazing activists, icons, and personalities inside this book, as well as those who couldn't be included. Thank you for your tireless work for fat bodies and the body positive/fat acceptance movements. We need you.
Thank you also to all my family, friends, and supporters who encouraged me in this project. It was something I needed to do for myself, and you helped me to do it.

CONTENTS

INTRODUCTION

Body Positivity. Fat Activism. Fat Acceptance. These movements are becoming more widespread as the days go on, but many people have never heard of them or even know what they mean. Body positivity differs from Fat Acceptance and Fat Activism in that Body Positivity is a generalized movement meant to spread the idea that all bodies are good bodies, that our worth should not be based on judgments about our bodies, large or small. Fat Acceptance and Fat Activism are more specific movements focusing on the oppression of fat bodies – how privileges and rights such as healthcare, childcare, lack of harassment, and general respect are doled out based on the perceived "health" of a person or on other judgments of their body size. These movements are fighting to have fat people gain equal rights and privileges, see more positive or neutral fat representation in the media, and to challenge what we think we know about fatness.

This colouring book was put together for my own personal journey towards self-love. The personalities, activists, and icons in the following pages are those who have inspired me to love my body as it is, to come to terms with the idea that I can live a full and happy life in a fat body, and to realize that nobody has the right to tell me differently or treat me badly based on this fact. I hope that you are as inspired and moved as I have been by the work of the people in this book.

For more information, please visit the personalities' websites and social media sites. They are listed on the back of each colouring page.

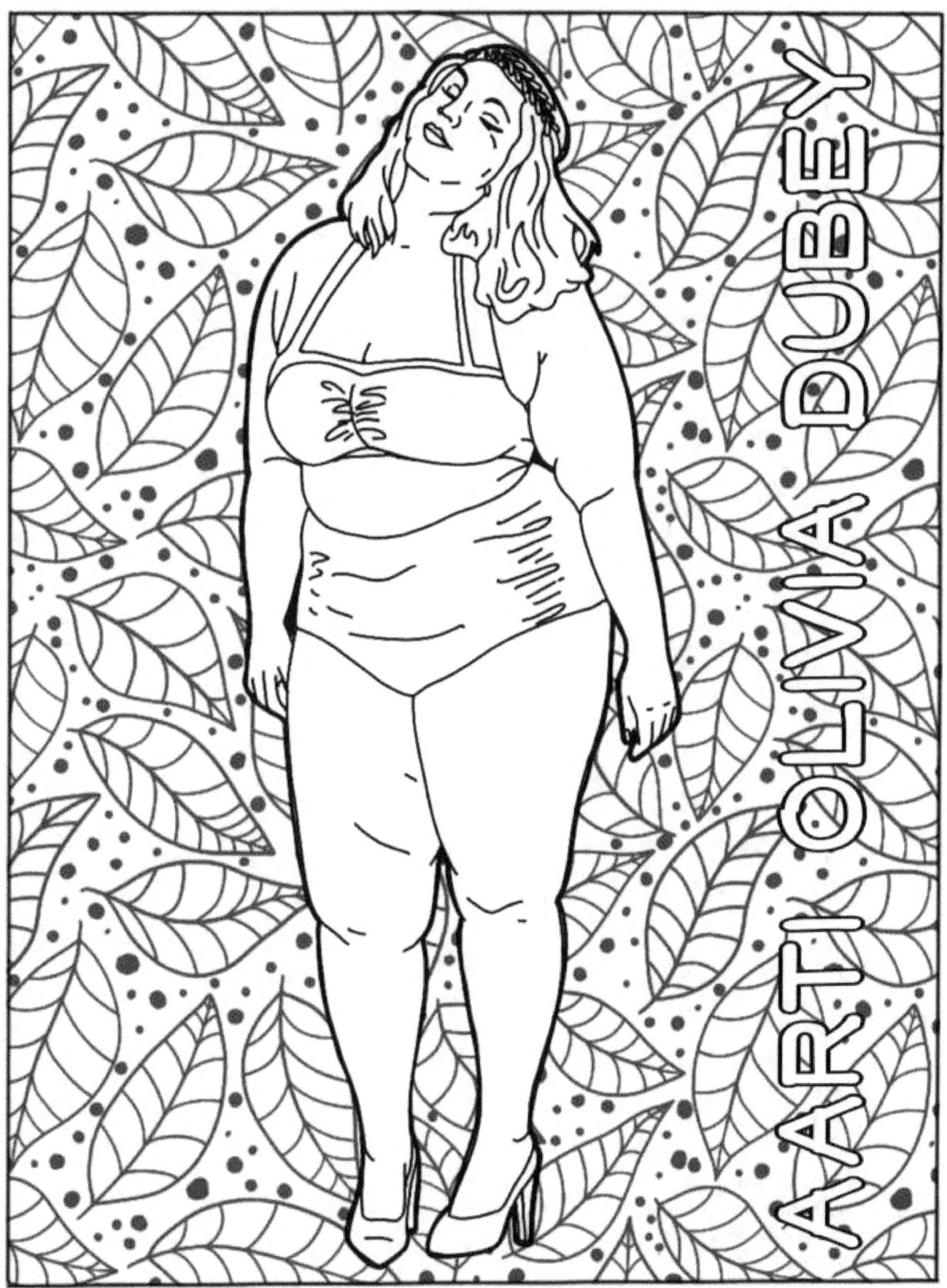

AARTI OLIVIA DUBEY

Aarti Olivia Dubey (they/she)
Digital Creator for Curves Become Her, Writer, Activist
www.linktr.ee/curvesbecomeher
IG: @curvesbecomeher

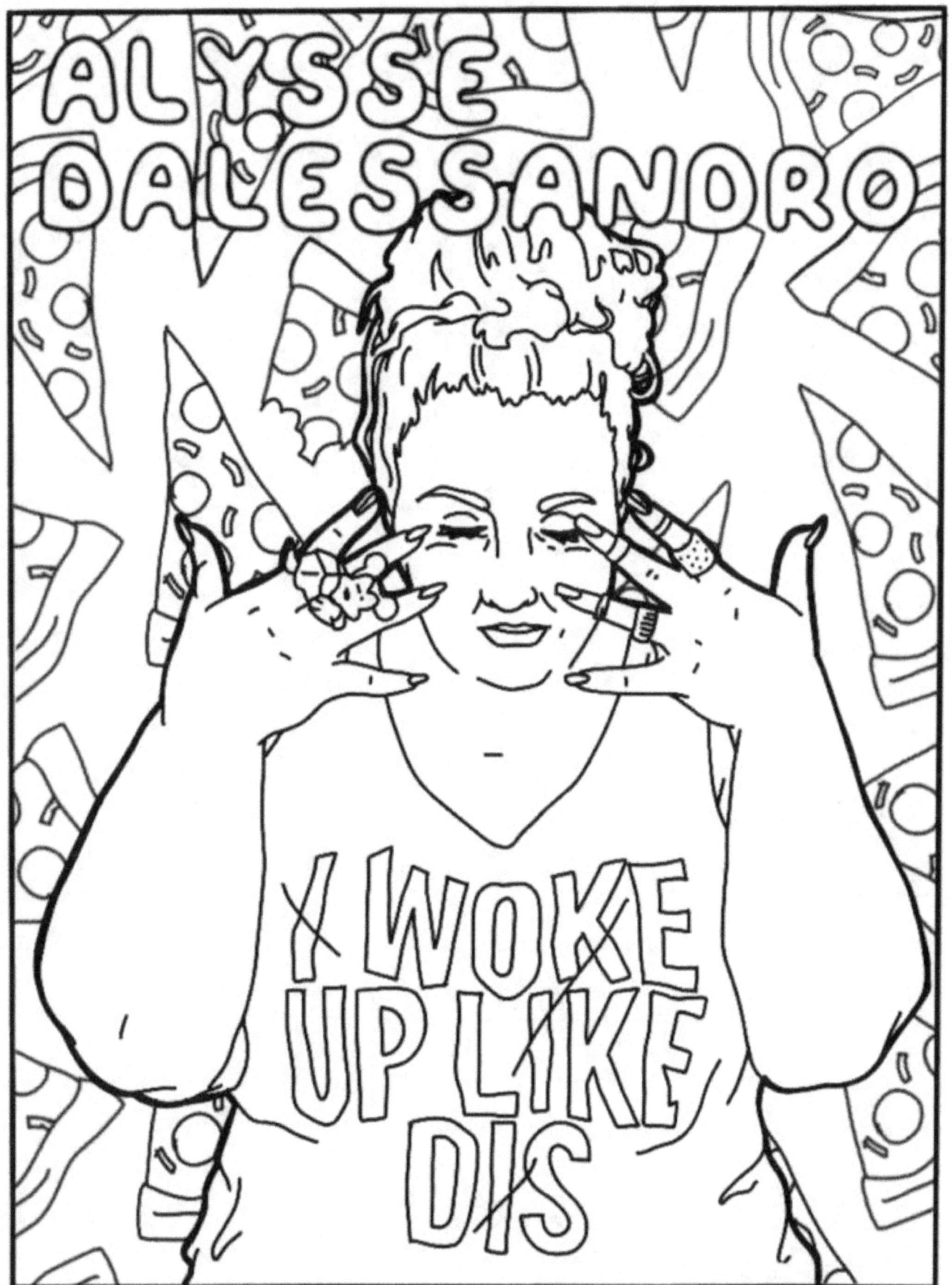

Alysse Dalessandro (she/her)
Digital Creator, Writer, Entreprenur, and Model
www.readytostare.com
IG: @ readytostare and @secondhandstare

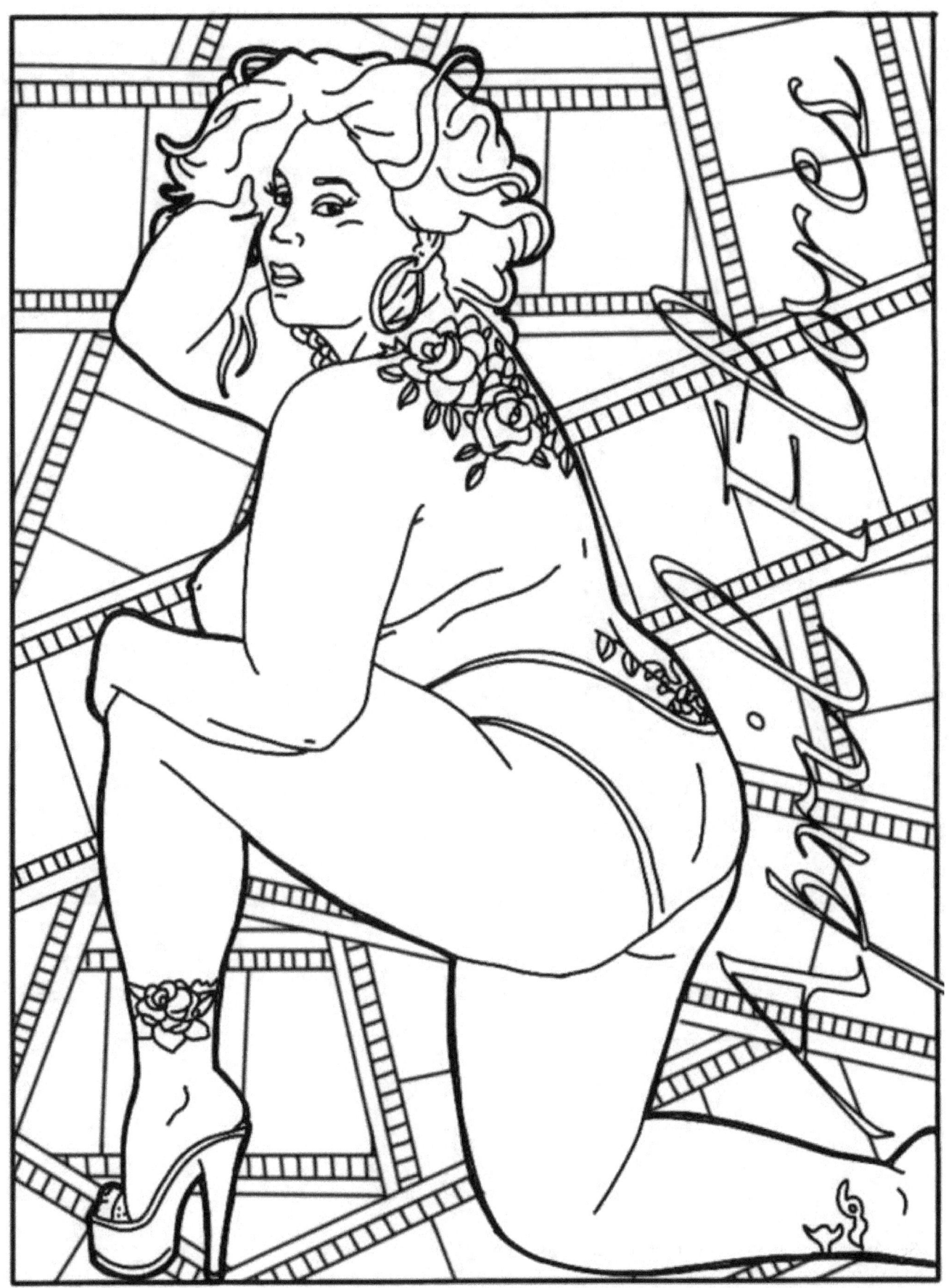

April Flores (she/her)
Sex Artist, Model, Writer, Activist and Certified Intimacy Coordinator
www.onlyaprilflores.com
Twitter: @theaprilflores

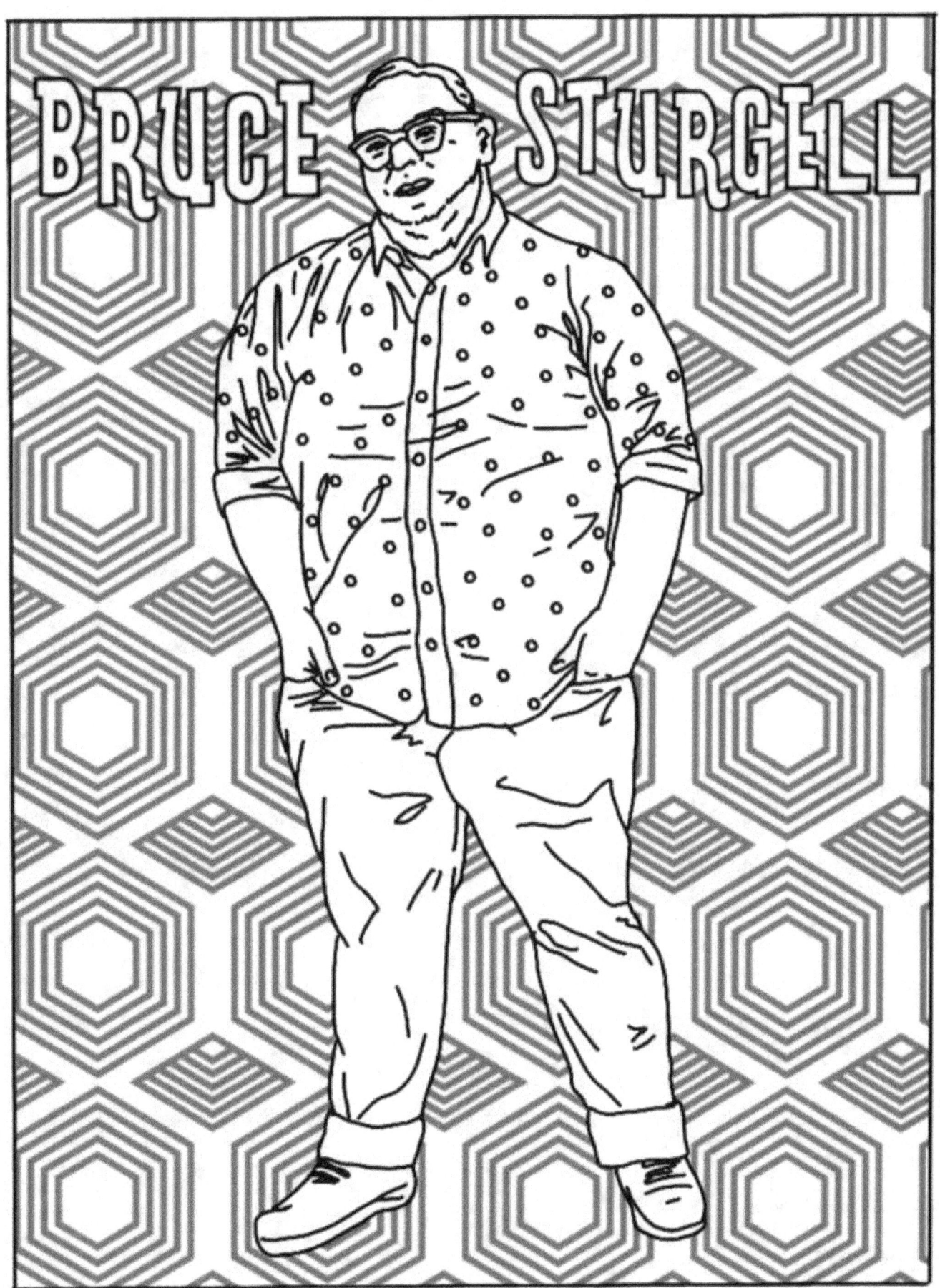

Bruce Sturgell (he/him)
Founder, Editor in Chief and Model for Chubstr.com
www.chubstr.com
IG: @chubstr

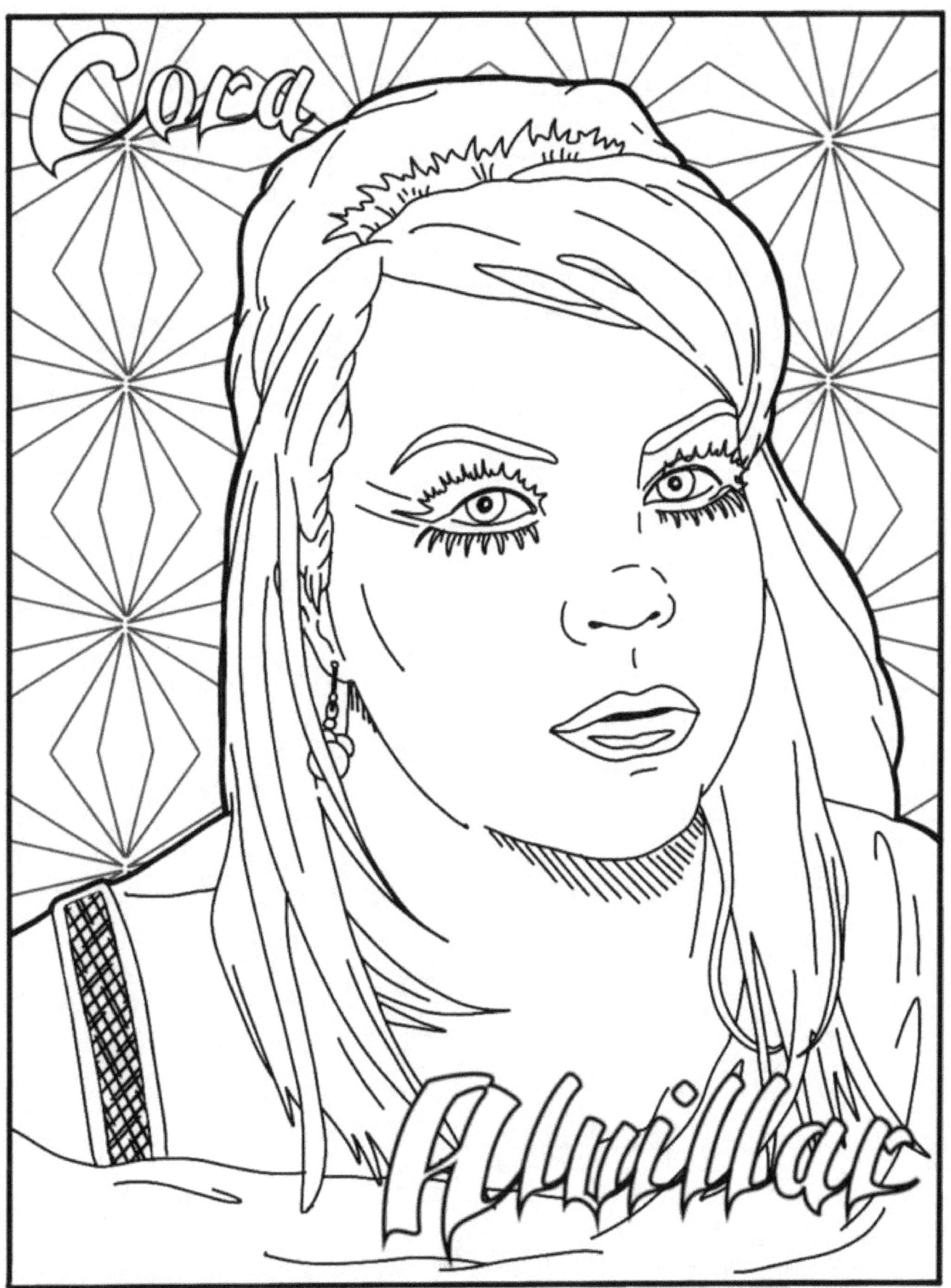

Cora Alvillar (she/her)
Freelance Makeup Artist, Fashion and Beauty Blogger for Vintage or Tacky
www.youtube.com/c/vintageortacky
IG: @vintageortacky

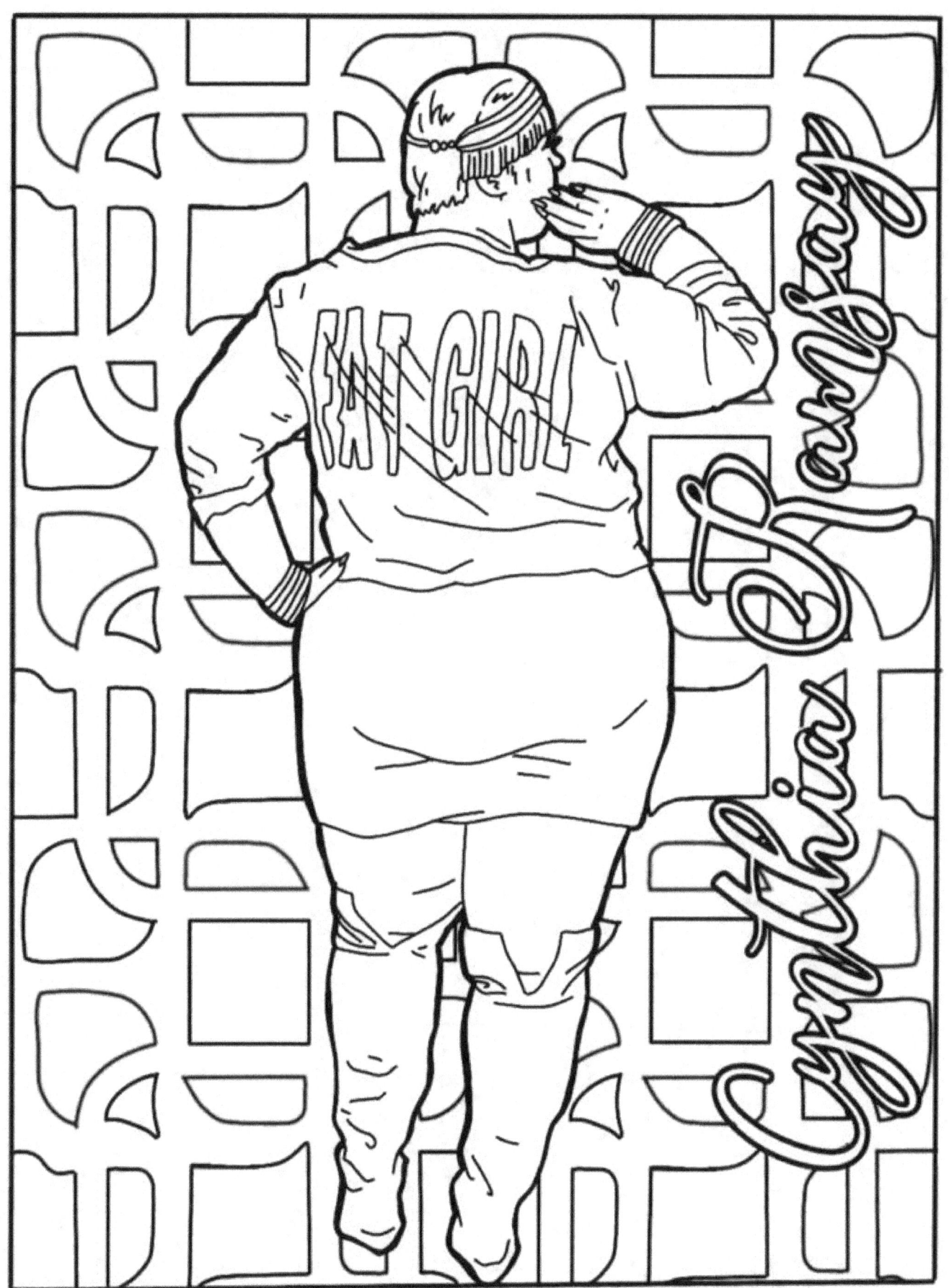

Cynthia Ramsay
Founder of Flight of the Fat Girl, Blogger, and Writer
https://flightofthefatgirl.wordpress.com/ *(no longer active)*

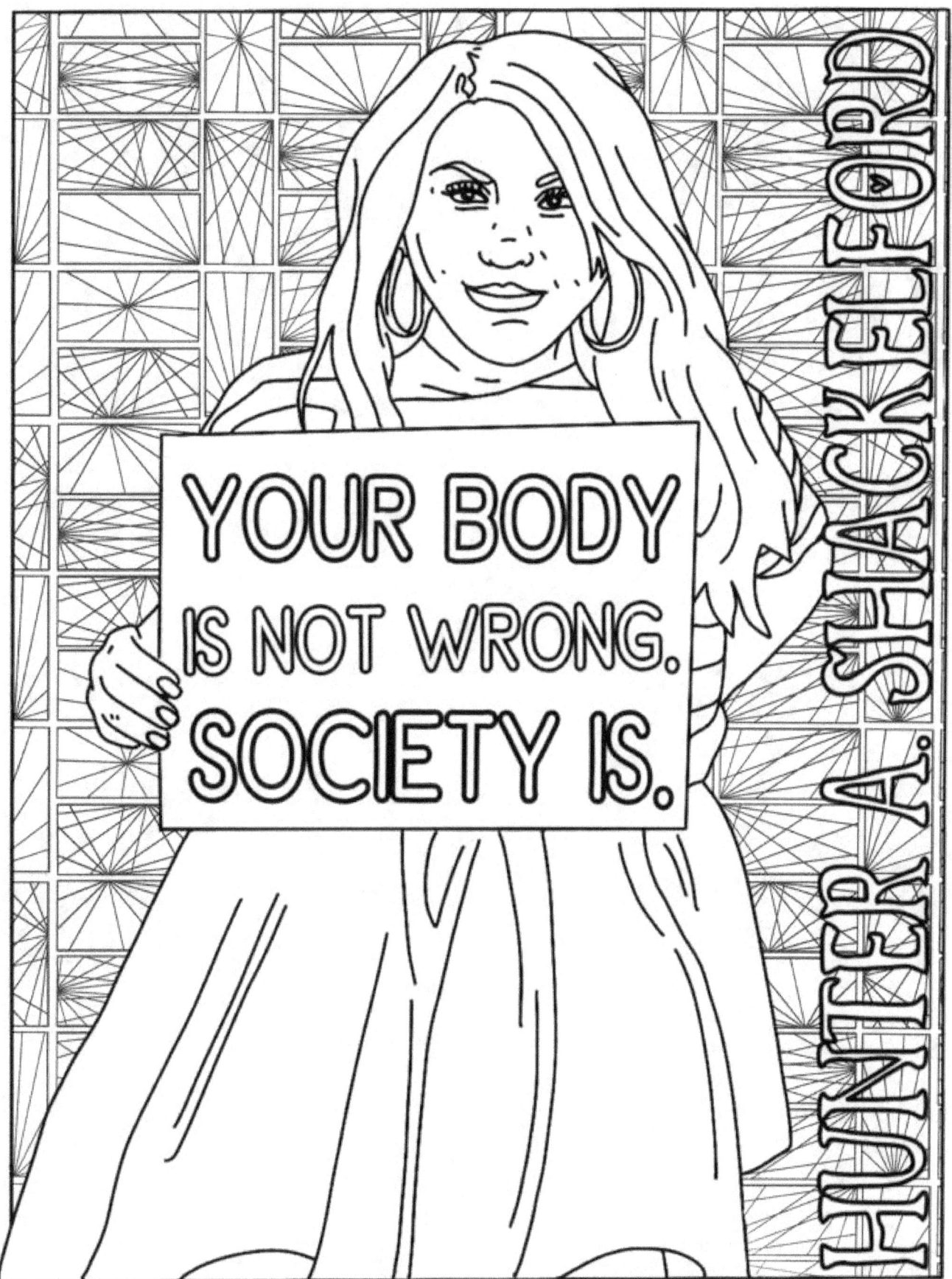

Hunter Shackelford (they/them)
Storyteller, Abolitionist, Death Worker
www.deathfeminism.com
IG: @huntythelion

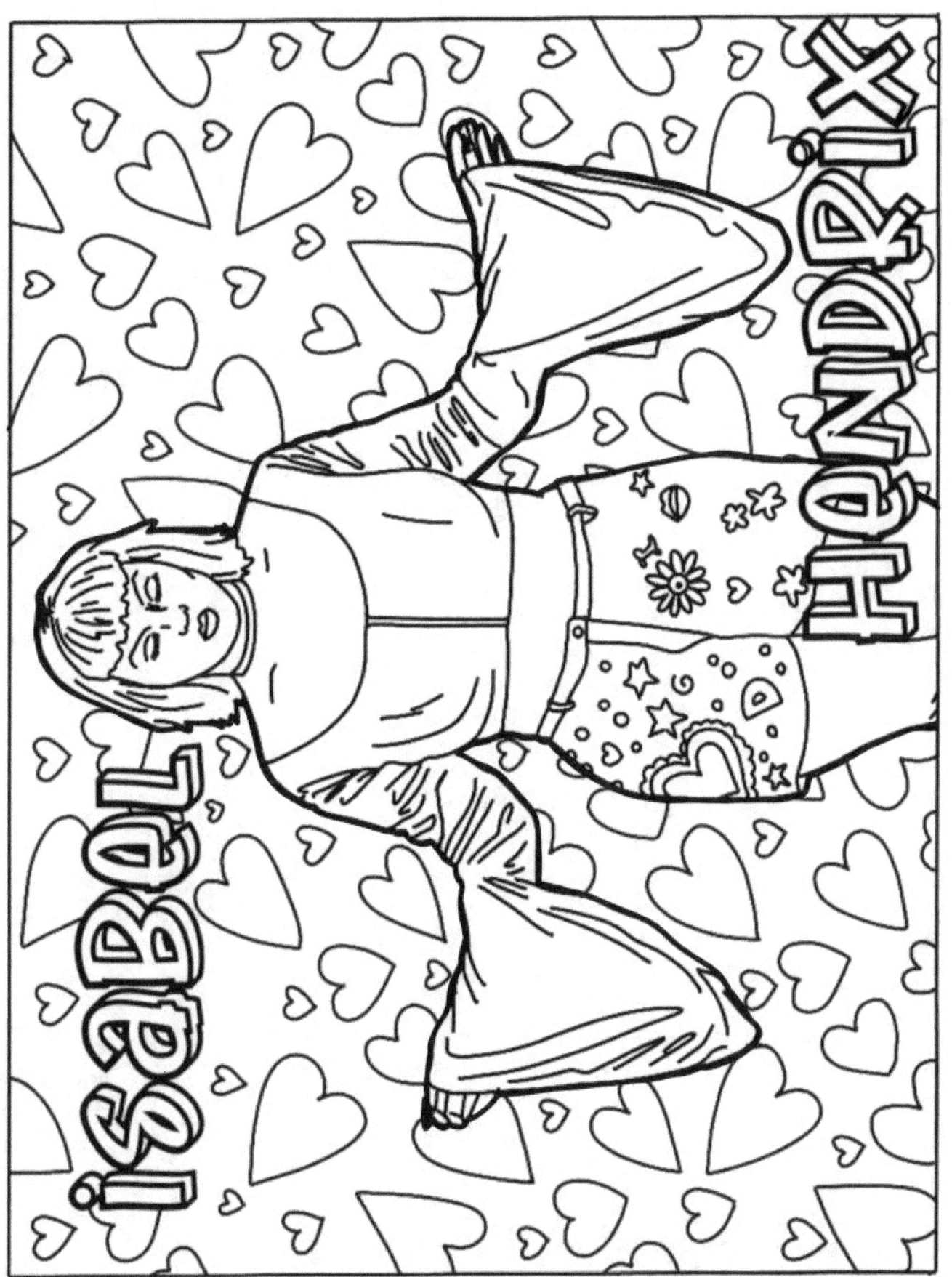

Isabel Hendrix (she/they)
Model, Digital Creator, Self-Love Advocate
www.linktr.ee/isabel_hendrix
IG: @isabel_hendrix

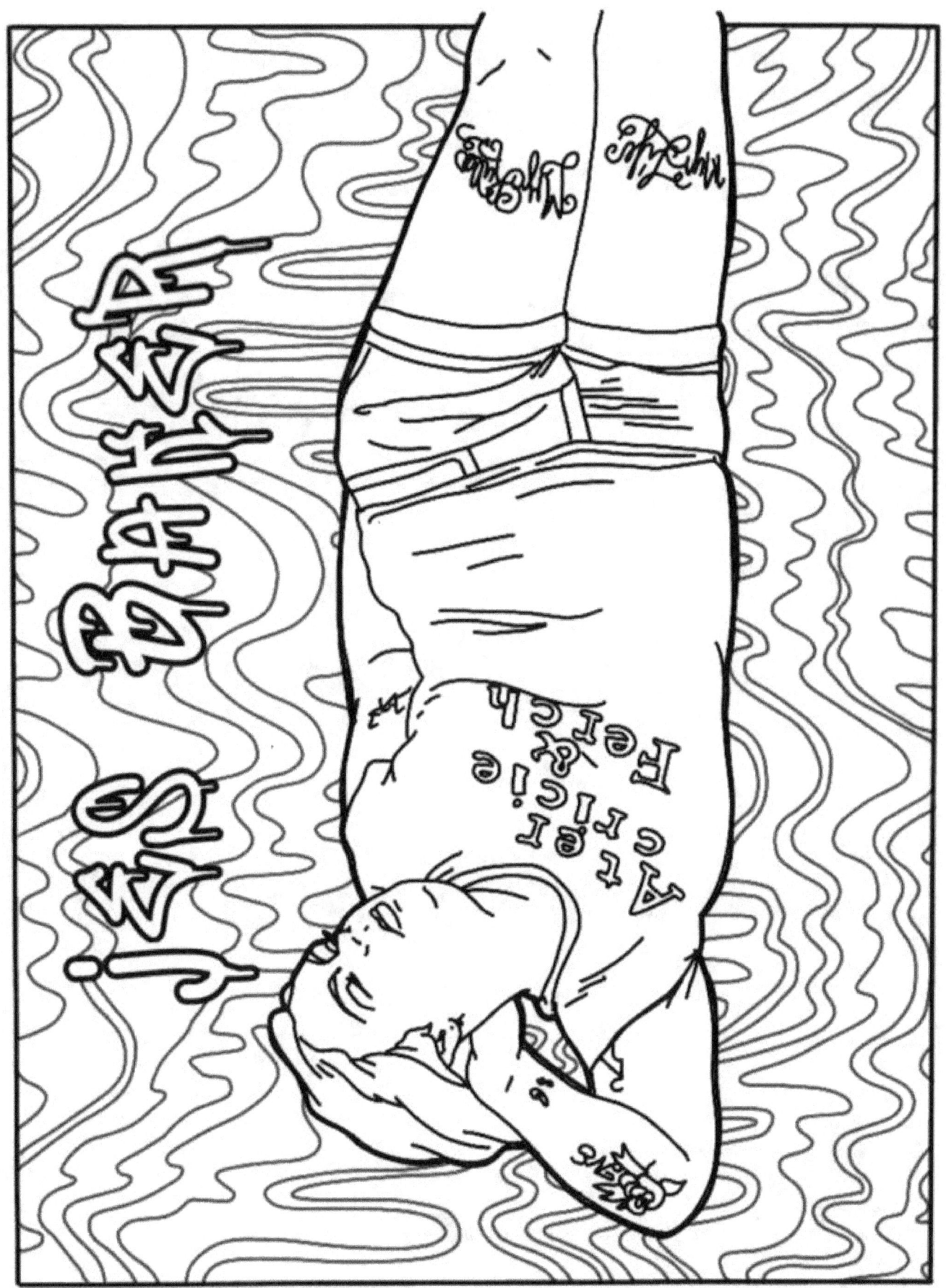

Jes Baker (she/they)
Author of *Things No One Will Tell Fat Girls* and *Land Whale*, Blogger, Coach
www.themilitantbaker.com
IG: @themilitantbaker

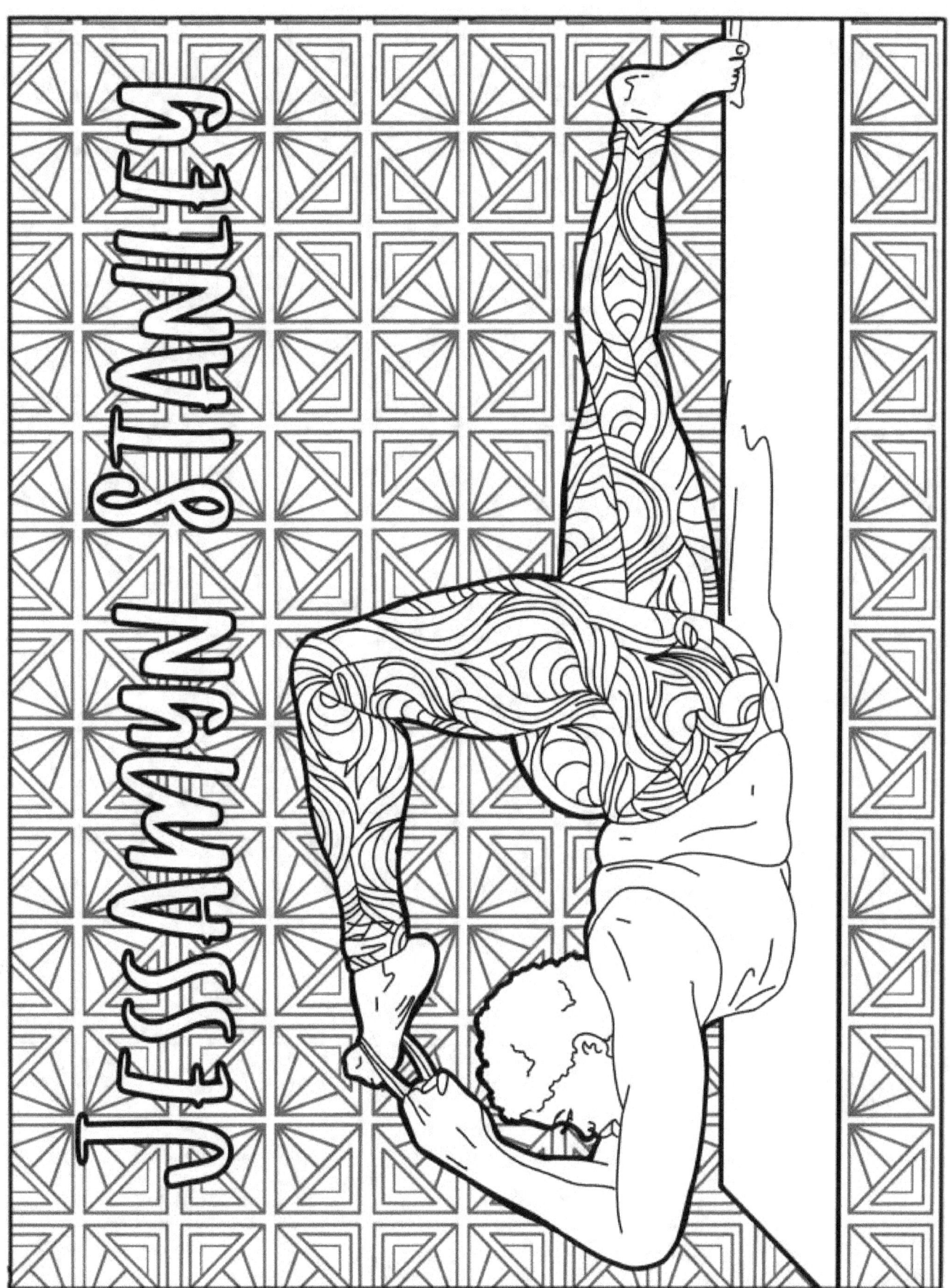

Jessamyn Stanley (she/her)
Author of *Yoke* and *Every Body Yoga*, Yoga Teacher, Entrepreneur and Advocate
www.jessamynstanley.com
IG: @mynameisjessamyn

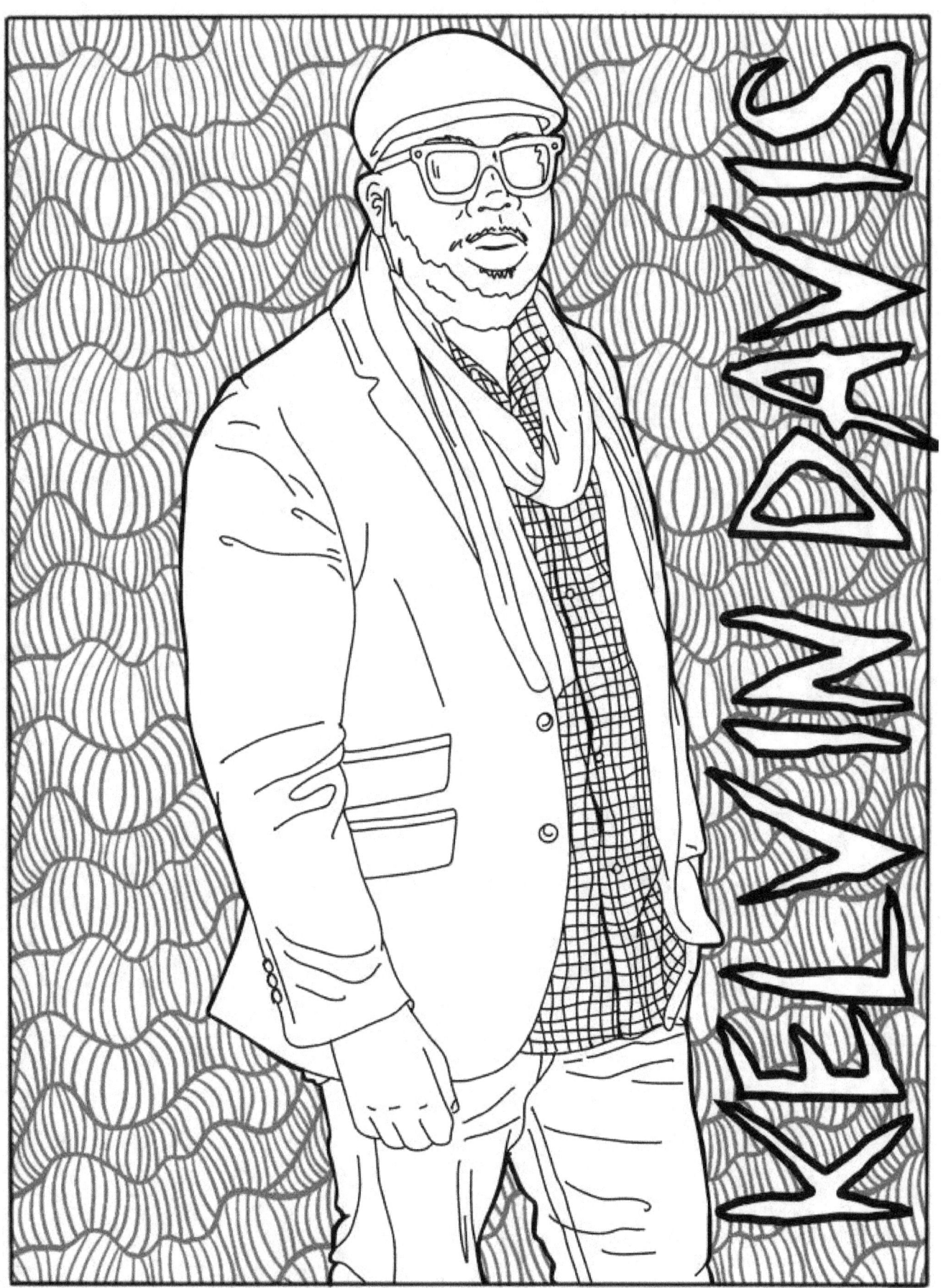

KELVIN DAVIS

Kelvin Davis (he/him)
Author, Model, Blogger, and Body Positive Advocate
www.linktr.ee/kelvindavis
IG: @kelvindavis

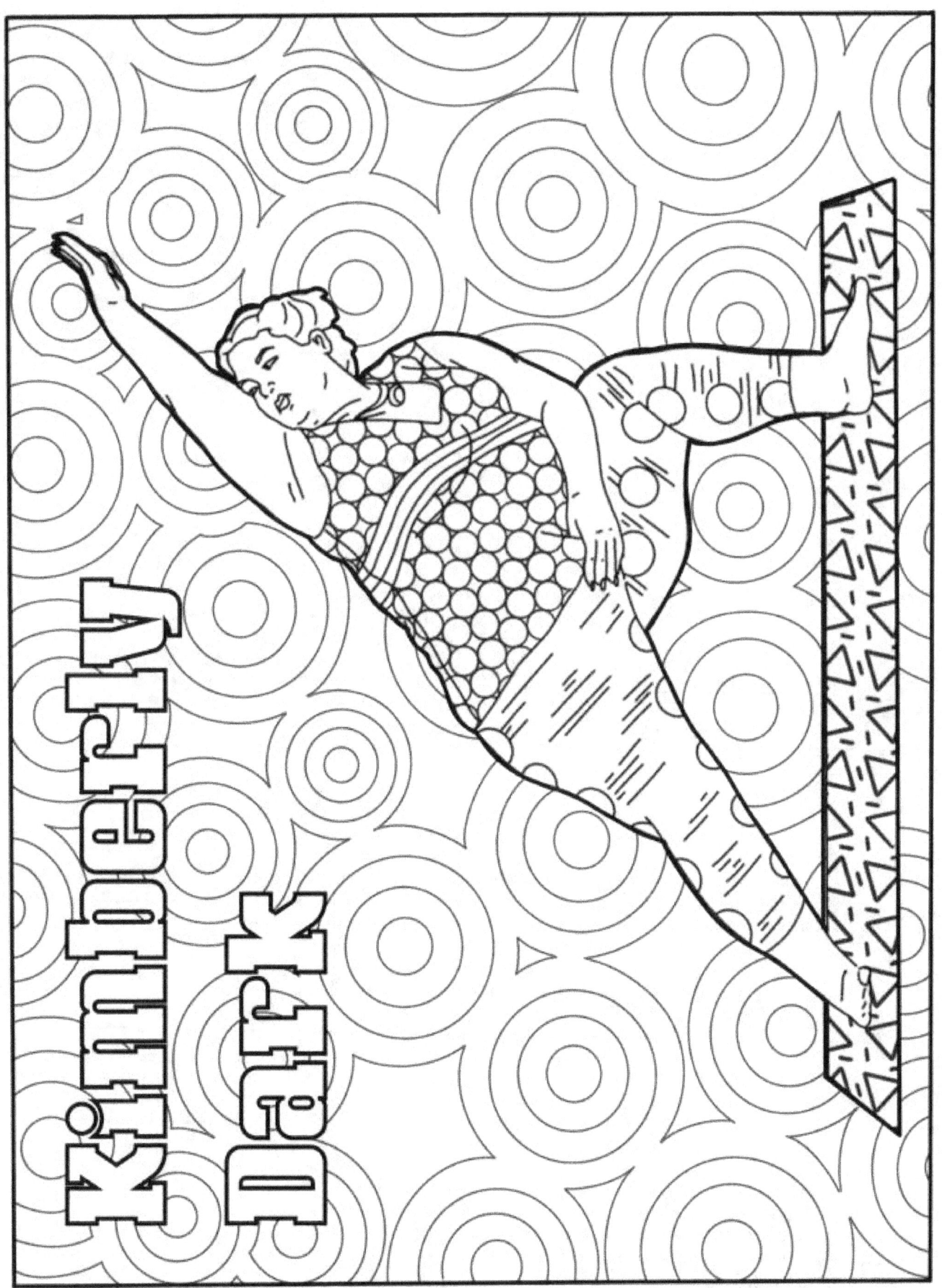

Kimberly Dark (she/her)
Author, Yoga Instructor, Professor, and Raconteur
www.linktr.ee/kimberlydark
IG: @kimberly.dark

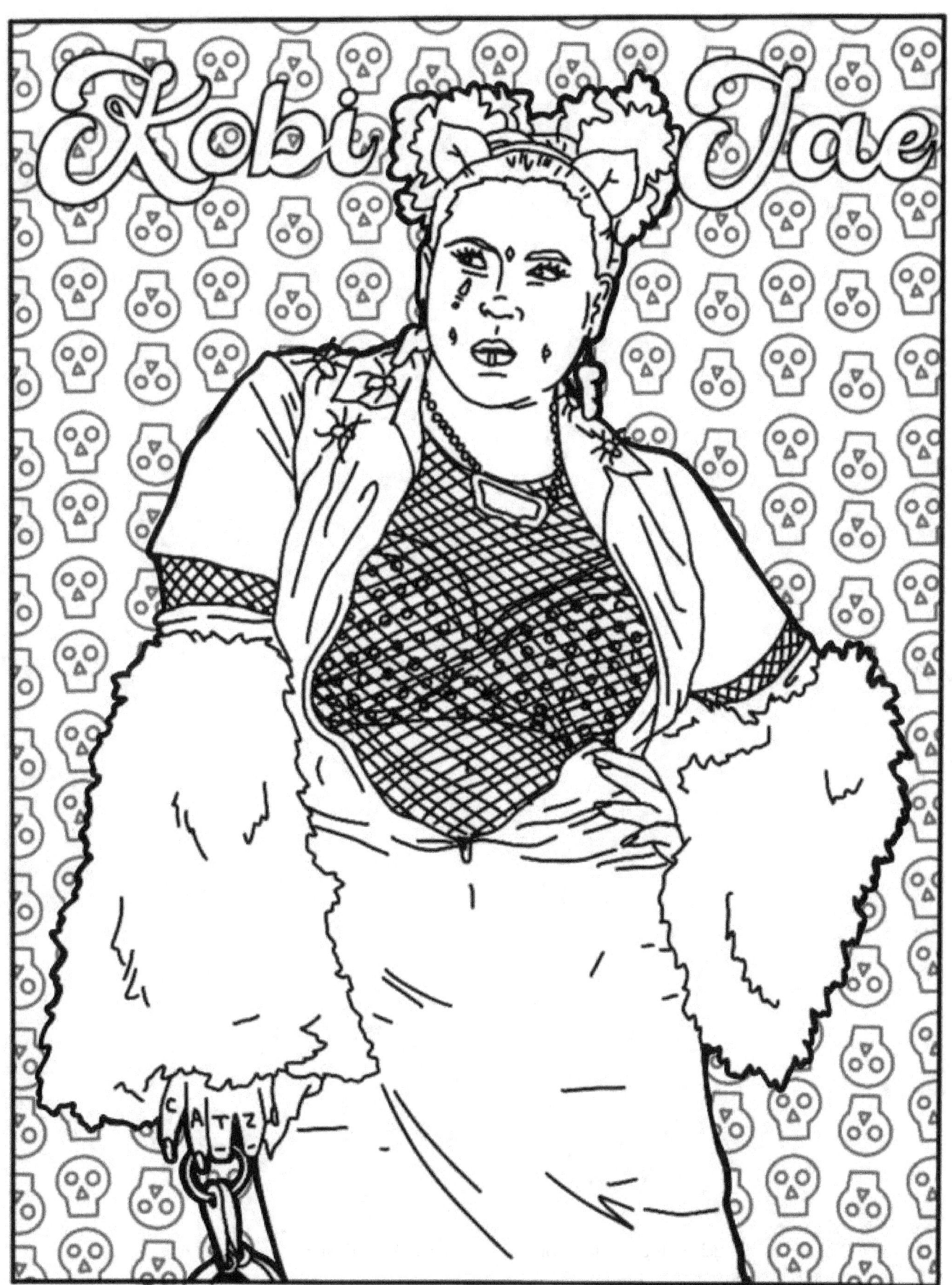

Kobi Jae (she/they)
Fashion Blogger and Model at Horror Kitsch Bitch, Graphic and Web Designer
www.horrorkitschbitch.com
IG: @kobi_jae

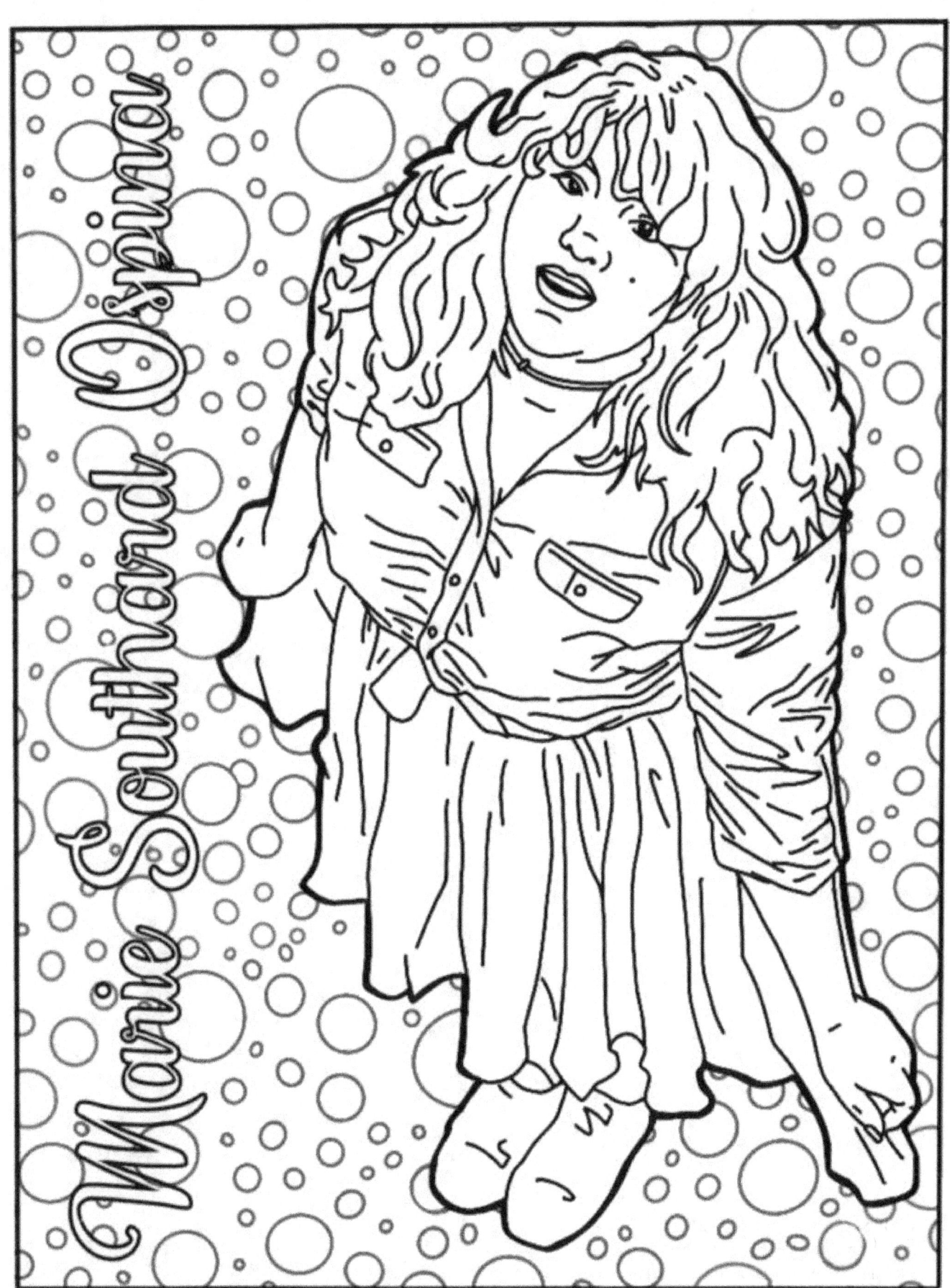

Marie Southard Ospina (she/her)
Writer and Blogger
www.linktr.ee/mariesouthardospina
IG: @mariesouthardospina

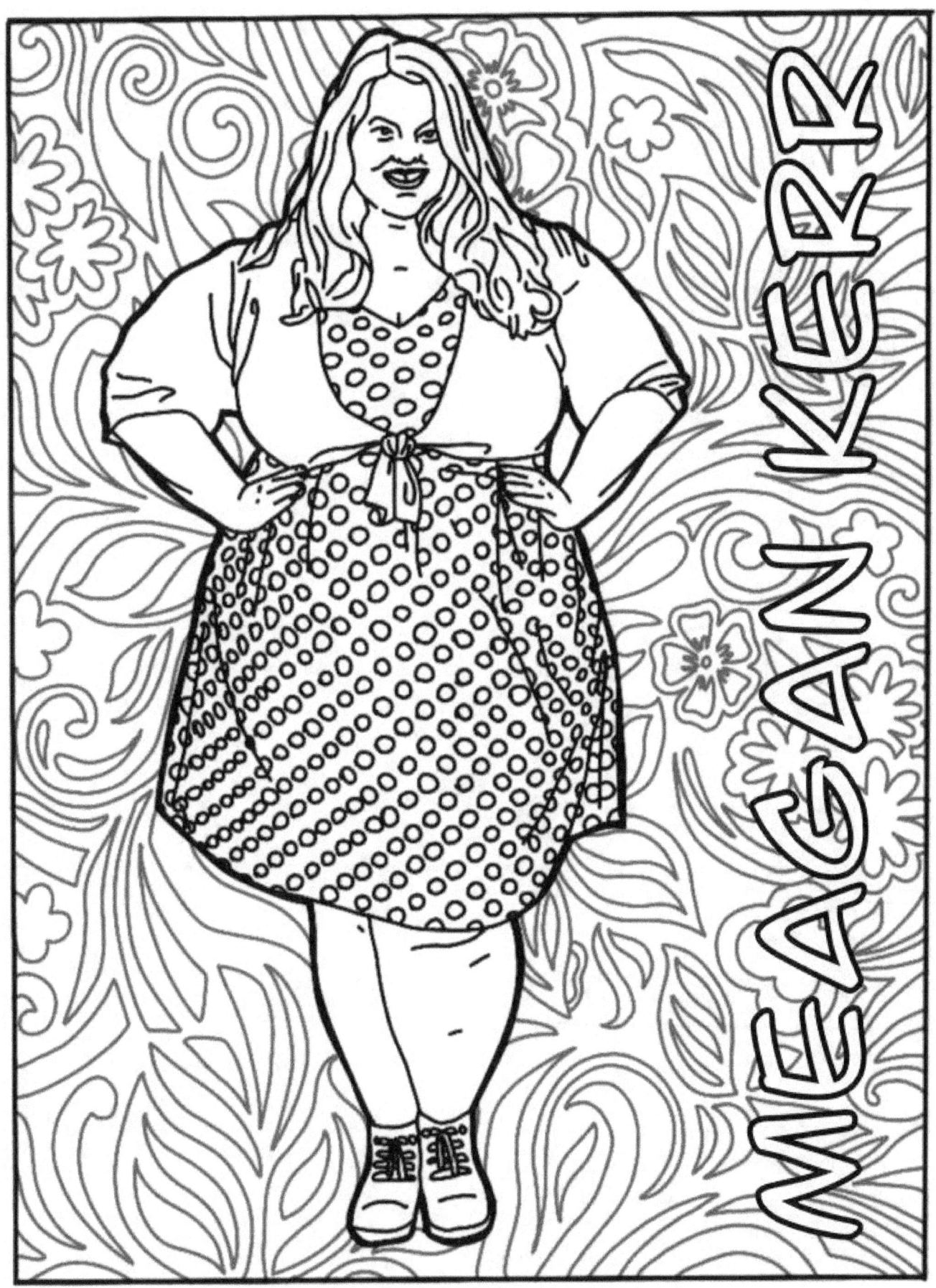

MEAGAN KERR

Meagan Kerr (she/her)
Plus-Size Fashion Blogger and Community Organizer
www.thisismeagankerr.com
IG: @thisismeagankerr

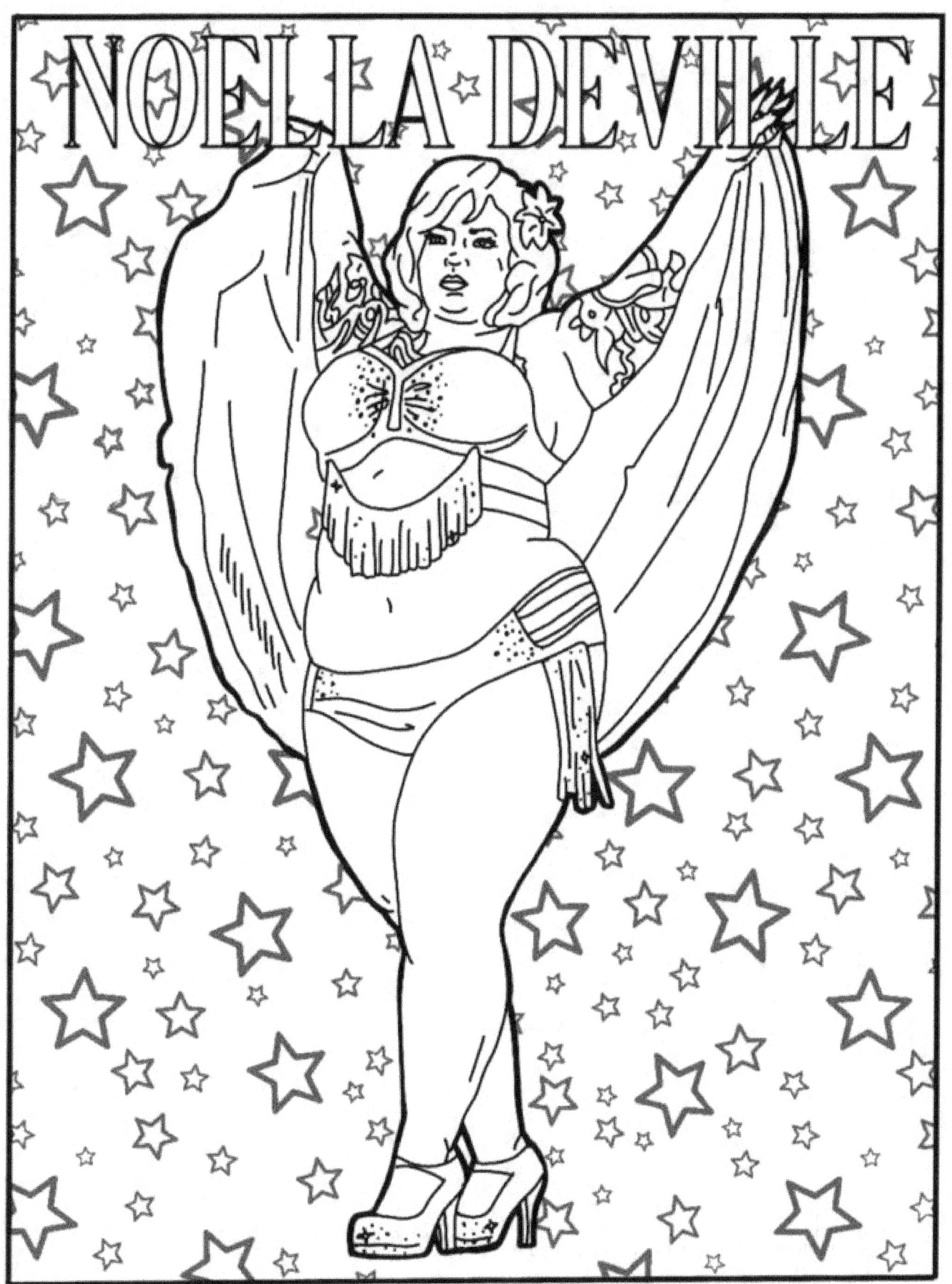

Noella DeVille (she/her)
Burlesque Performer, Fashion Model, and Body Positive Activist
www.linktr.ee/NoellaDeVille
IG: @noella_deville

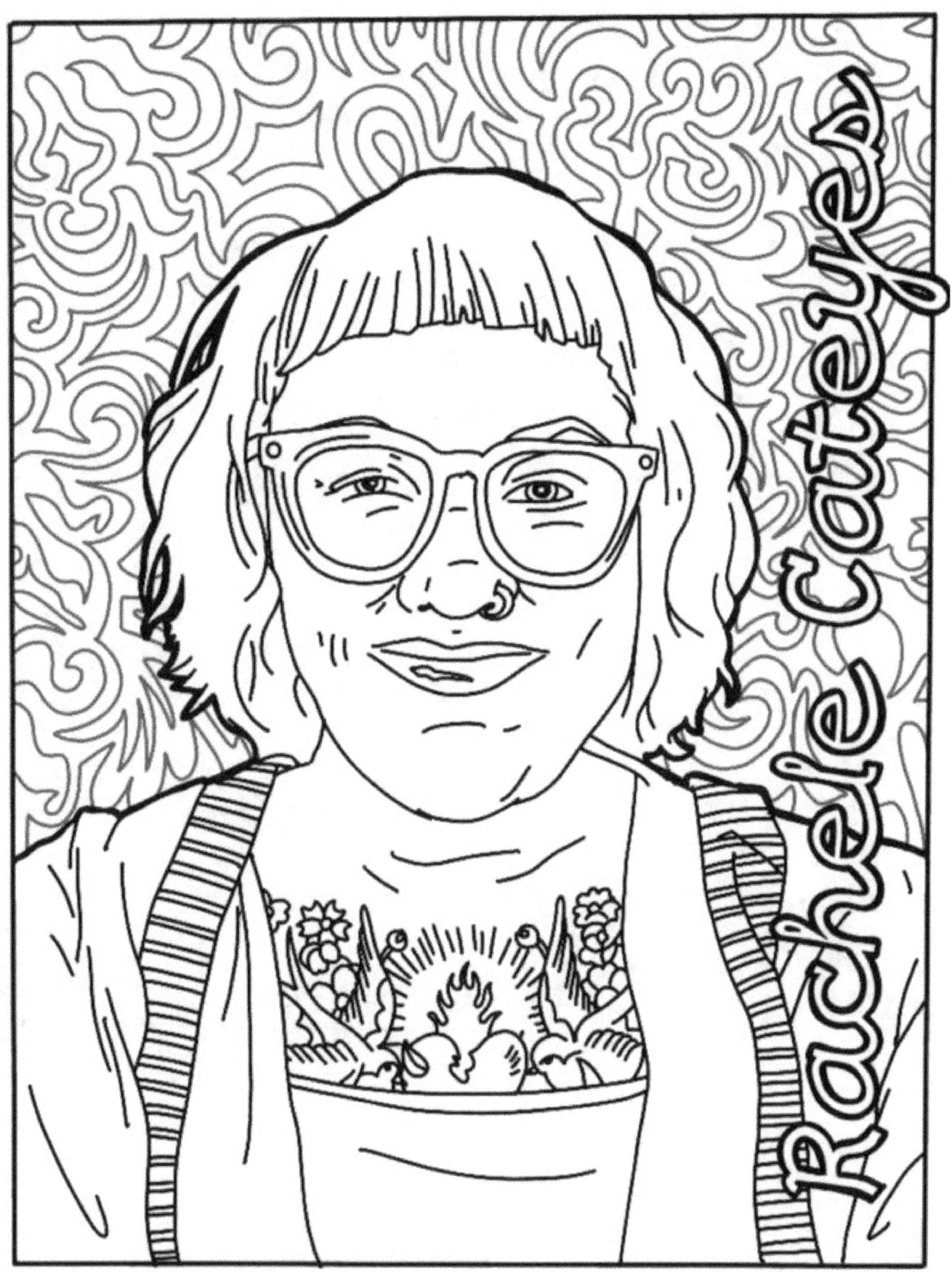

Rachele Cateyes
Body Positive Artist and Illustrator, Founder of Glorifying Obesity
www.rachelecateyes.weebly.com *(no longer active)*

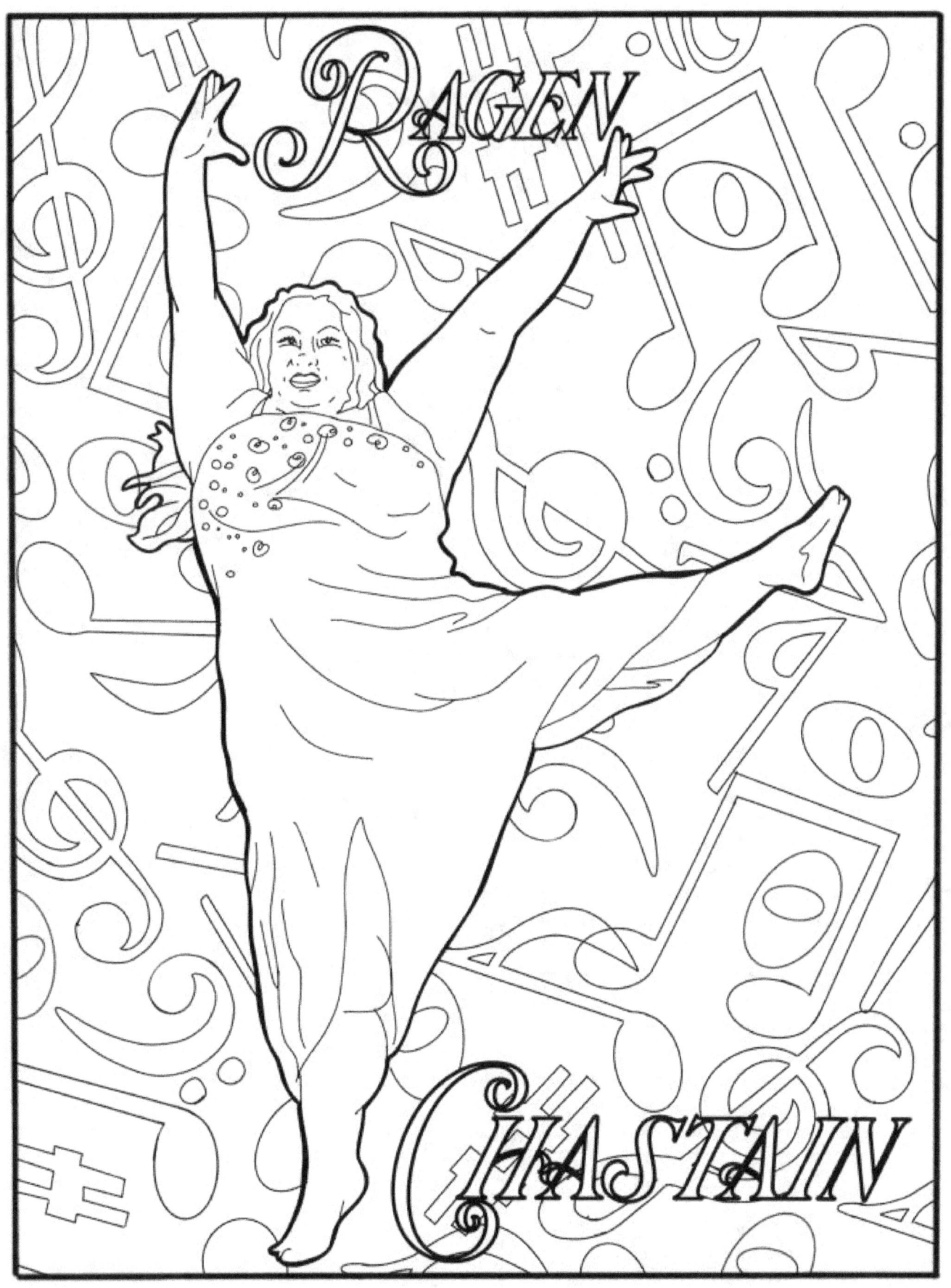

Ragen Chastain (she/her)
Speaker, Writer, Activist, Researcher, and Athlete
www.danceswithfat.org and https://weightandhealthcare.substack.com/
IG: @ragenchastain

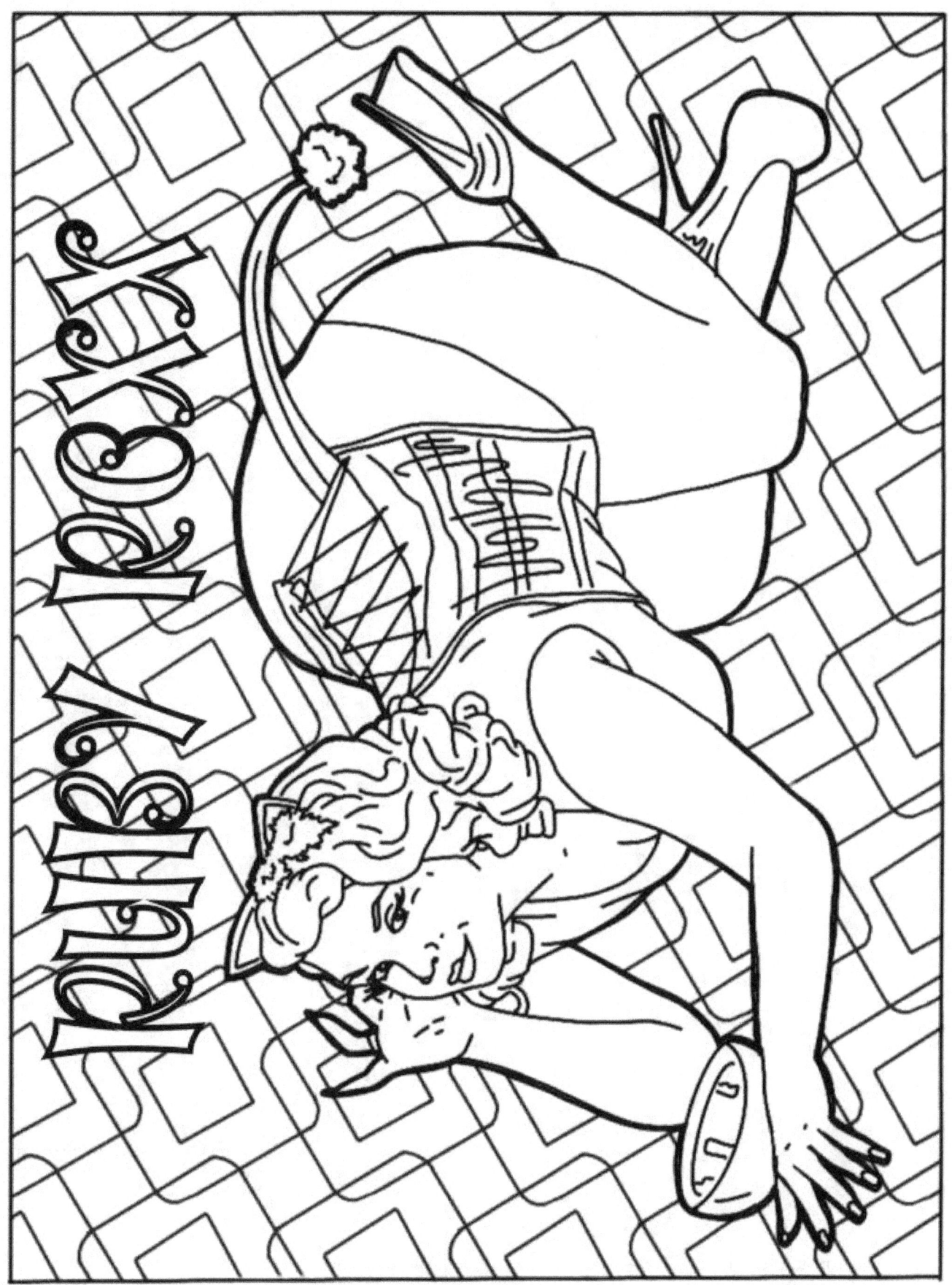

Ruby Roxx
Model, Blogger, and Influencer
www.rubyroxxmodel.com
Twitter: @vanrubyroxx

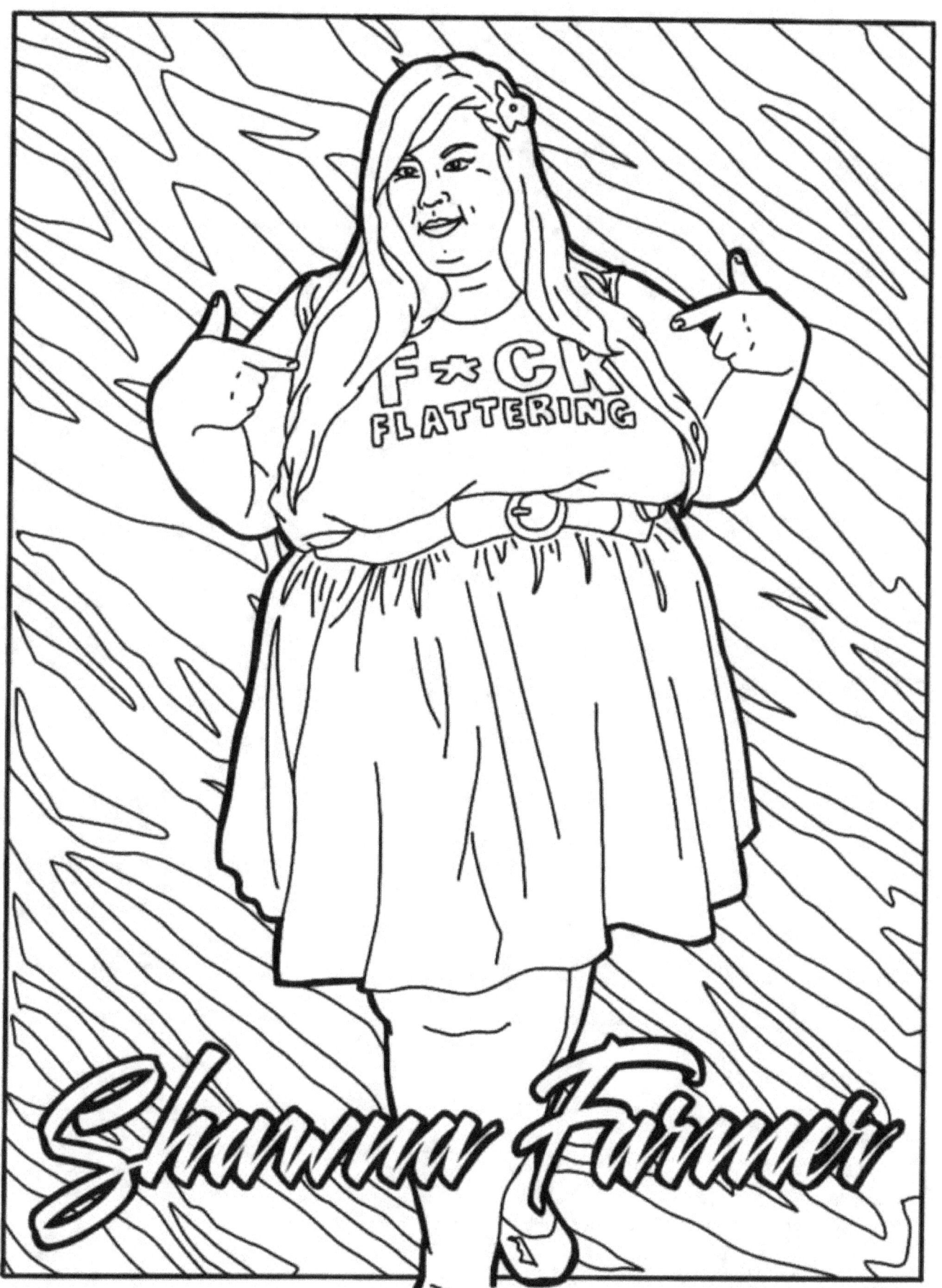

Shawna Farmer (she/her)
Former Owner, Designer, and Model for Chubby Cartwheels (*no longer active*), Digital Content Creator
www.linktr.ee/shawnapdx
IG: @chubbycartwheels

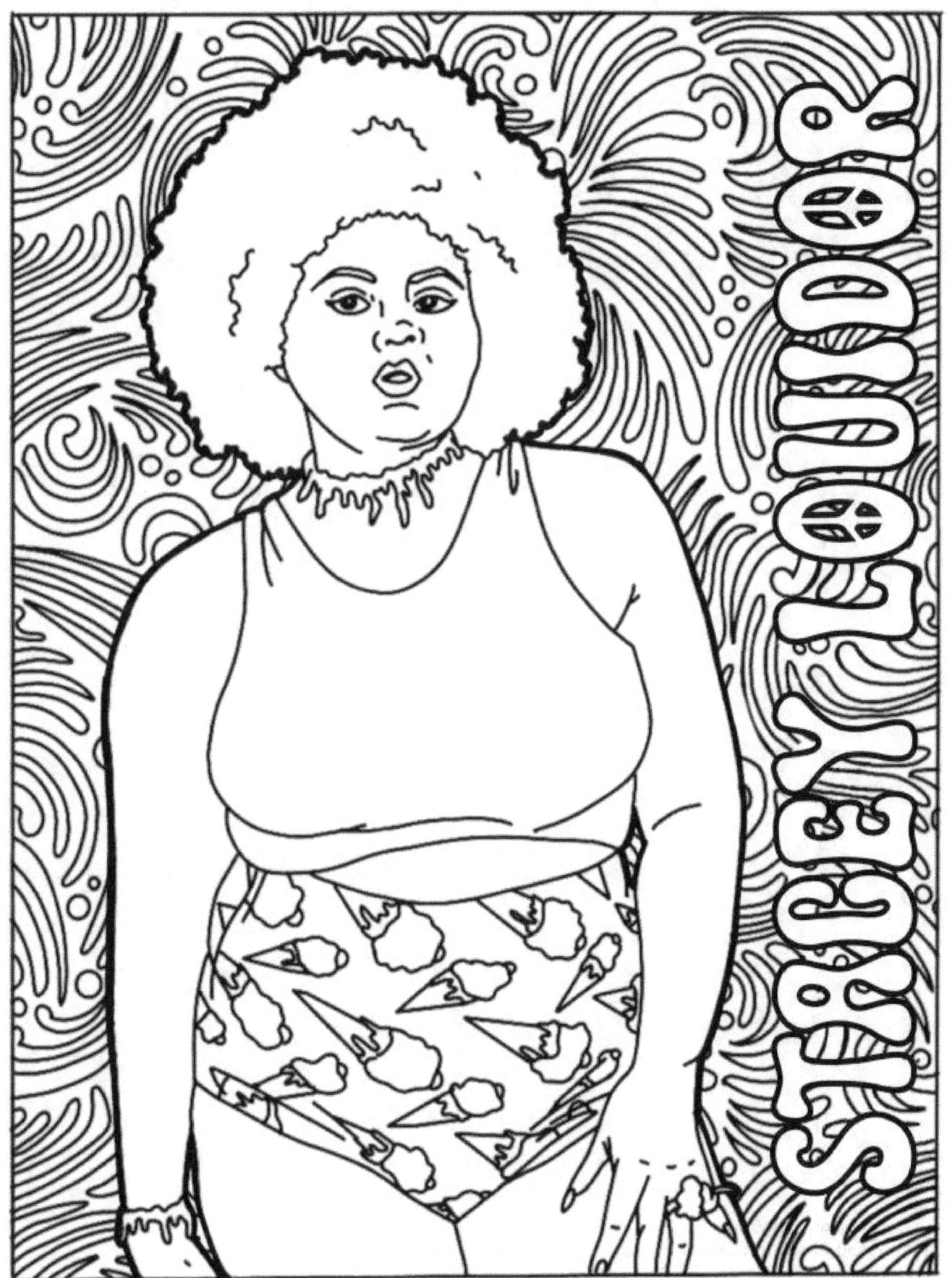

Stacey Louidor (she/her)
Model and Alternative Fashion Blogger at Hantise De L'oubli
IG: @hantisedeloubli

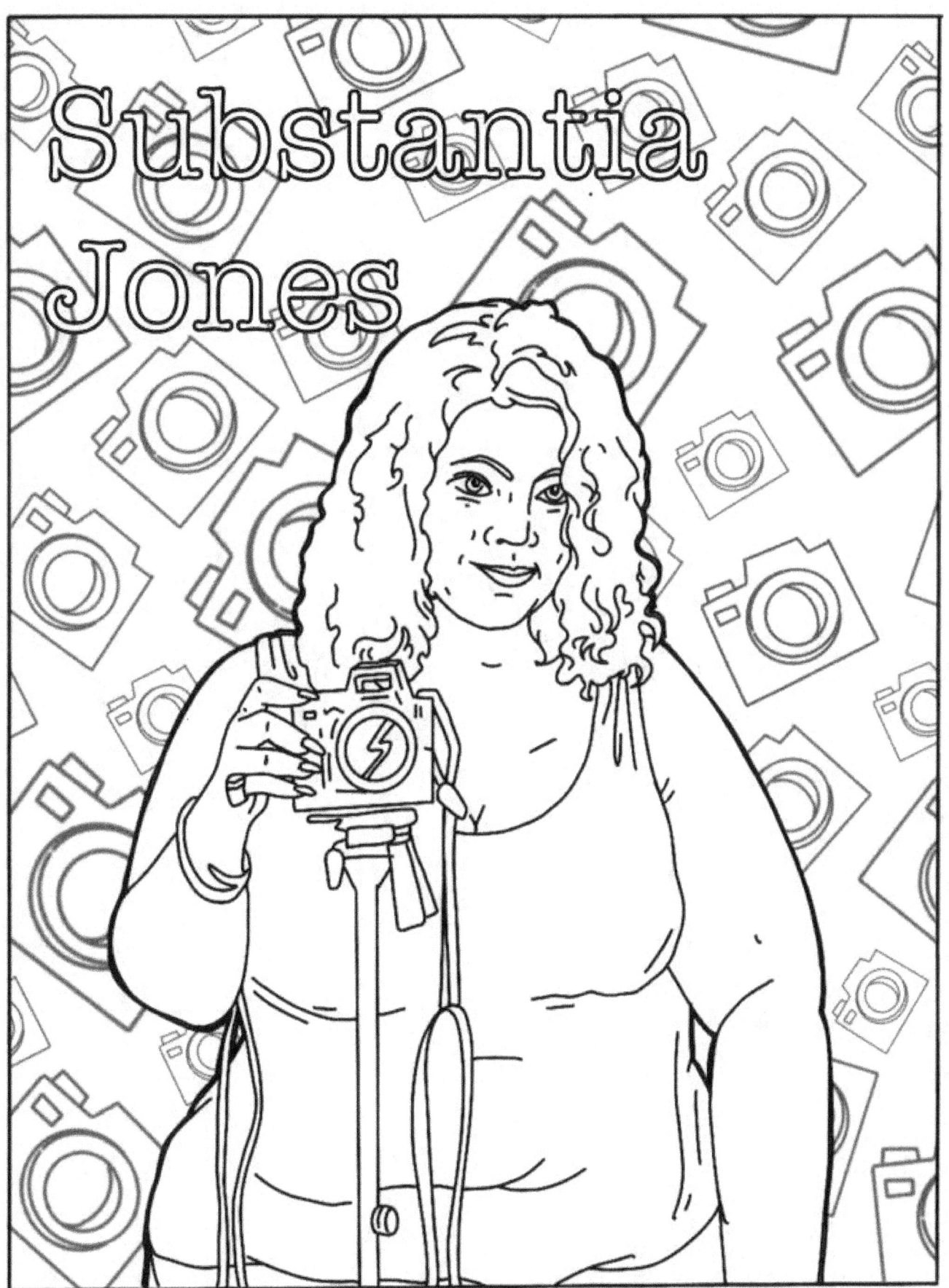

Substantia Jones

Substantia Jones (she/her)
Photoactivist and Founder of the Adipositivity Project
www.adipositivity.com
IG: @adipositivity

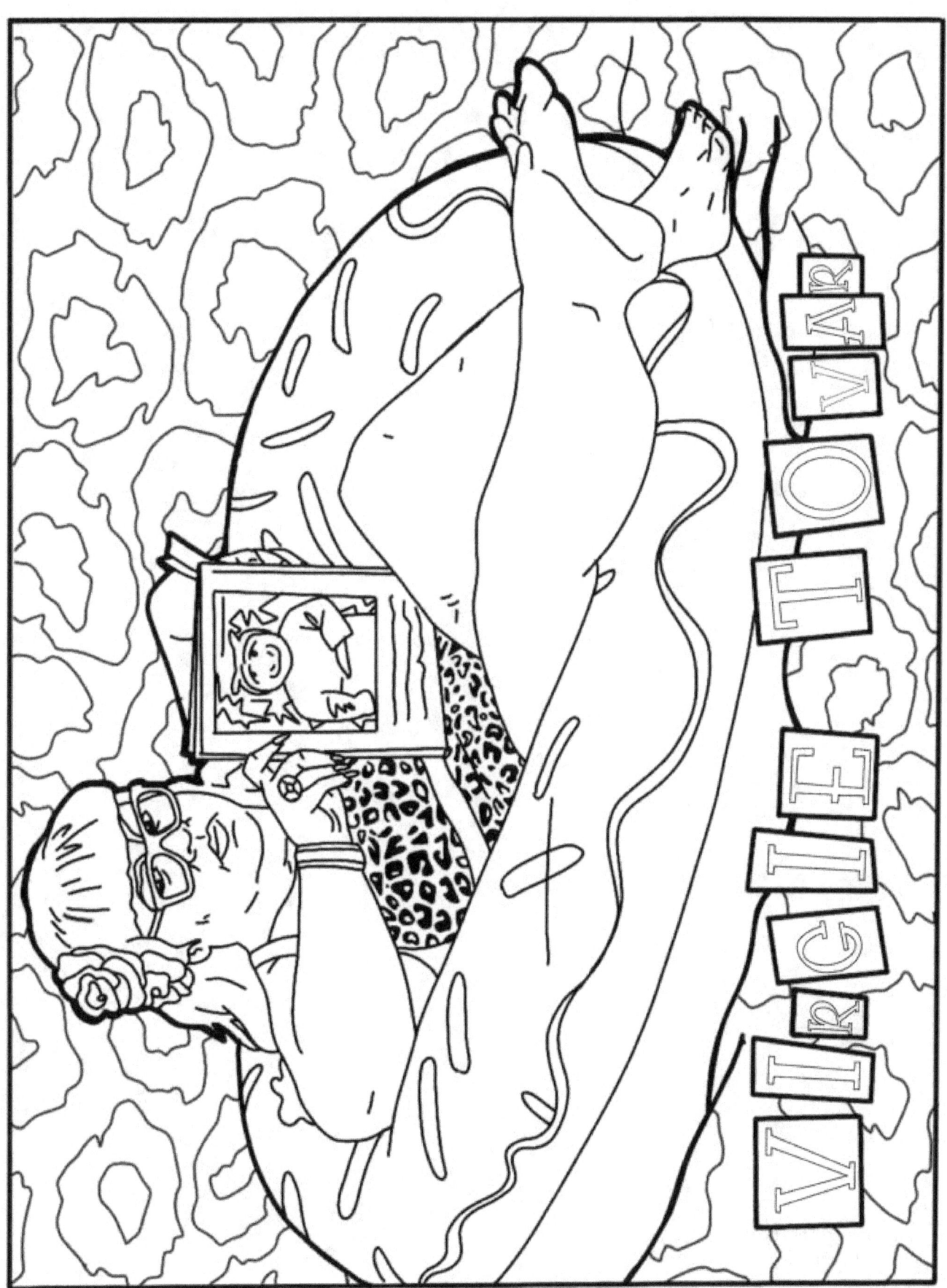

Virgie Tovar (she/her)
Author, Lecturer,
www.virgietovar.com
IG: @virgietovar

ABOUT THE AUTHOR

Allison Tunis (she/they) is a fat, queer, disabled artist living and working on Treaty 6 territory, in amiswaciwâskahikan (Edmonton, AB, Canada). Allison uses her education in visual arts and art therapy, combined with her personal experiences as a community organizer and self-advocate to explore themes of personal and community healing through the art creation process. They also look to challenge norms and expectations around marginalized bodies – with a specific focus on queer, fat, neurodivergent, and disabled experiences. Tunis aims to reimagine art materials, techniques, and collaborative processes in ways that reduce barriers and harm, while contributing to critical conversation within and beyond traditional art spaces about accessibility, intersectionality, social justice, and strengths-based theory.

Find more art from Allison at www.AllisonTunis.com

www.ingramcontent.com/pod-product-compliance
Lightning Source LLC
Chambersburg PA
CBHW081305180526
45170CB00007B/2566